W9-BFA-323

The • Life Cycle • Series

The Life Cycle of a
SEA TURTLE

Bobbie Kalman

Crabtree Publishing Company

www.crabtreebooks.com

The Life Cycle Series

A Bobbie Kalman Book

For Gina and Simplicio,
our dear friends in Honolulu

Editor-in-Chief
Bobbie Kalman

Editors
Kathryn Smithyman
Niki Walker
Amanda Bishop

Cover design
Kymberley McKee Murphy

Computer design
Campbell Creative Services

Production coodinator
Heather Fitzpatrick

Photo research
Karuna Thal
Heather Fitzpatrick

Consultant
Patricia Loesche, Ph.D., Animal Behavior
Program, Department of Psychology,
University of Washington

Special thanks to: Lindsey Potter,
Michael Nolan, Robert Thomas,
Karuna Thal, and Dolphin Quest

Photographs
Frank S. Balthis: page 12
Bobbie Kalman: pages 21 (bottom), 31 (both); bottom photo taken at
    Dolphin Quest at the Kahala Mandarin Oriental Hawaii Hotel
© Maris & Marilyn Kazmers/Seapics.cm: page 28
Michael S. Nolan: page 29
© Doug Perrine/Seapics.com: pages 10, 13, 18, 19, 20, 23 (insert), 27
Tom Stack and Associates: Ann Duncan: page 30;
    Barbara Gerlach: page 14;
    Chip Isenhart: page 15
© Masa Ushioda/Seapics.com: page 21 (top)
Other images by Digital Vision

Illustrations
Barbara Bedell: pages 4, 16-17 (bottom)
Patrick Ching: central front cover image, page 11
Margaret Amy Reiach: series logo, front and back covers, title page,
    pages 5 (top), 6-7 (background), 16 (top left and right),
    19, 22-23 (bottom)
Bonna Rouse: pages 5 (middle and bottom), 6-7 (sea turtles), 12 (middle),
    13 (bottom), 15, 17 (top left and right), 21, 29
Robert Thomas: pages 3, 9 (top), 20 (bottom), 24-25, 26 (bottom)
Tiffany Wybouw: pages 8, 9 (bottom), 13 (top), 17 (middle left and right),
    18, 22 (top and inset), 24 (left), and all small turtles around headings

Crabtree Publishing Company

www.crabtreebooks.com   1-800-387-7650

Cataloging-in-Publication Data
Kalman, Bobbie.
    The life cycle of a sea turtle / Bobbie Kalman
        p. cm. -- (The life cycle)
        Includes index.
    Describes how sea turtles develop from eggs to adult turtles and
migrate long distances, talks about the dangers they face from animal
and human predators, and suggests ways children can help.
    ISBN 0-7787-0652-4 (RLB) -- ISBN 0-7787-0682-6 (pbk.)
    1. Sea Turtles--Life cycles--Juvenile literature. [1. Sea turtles. 2. Turtles.
3. Endangered species.] I. Title.
    QL666.C536 K35 2002
    597.92'8--dc21
                                                        2001037213

**Published in
the United States**
PMB 16A
350 Fifth Ave.
Suite 3308
New York, NY
10118

**Published
in Canada**
616 Welland Ave.
St. Catharines, Ontario
L2M 5V6

**Published in the
United Kingdom**
White Cross Mills
High Town, Lancaster
LA1 4XS

**Published
in Australia**
386 Mt. Alexander Rd.
Ascot Vale (Melbourne)
VIC 3032

Contents

Sea turtles are reptiles

Turtles are **reptiles**. All reptiles have scales and a backbone, and they breathe with lungs. They are **cold-blooded** animals. Their body temperatures change as their surroundings become warmer or cooler. The body temperatures of **warm-blooded** animals do not change with their surroundings.

Some reptiles live on land, and others live in water. There are four main groups of reptiles:
1. alligators and crocodiles
2. tortoises, turtles, and sea turtles
3. tuataras
4. lizards and snakes

Turtles and sea turtles belong to the same reptile group as tortoises. Tortoises live only on land.

Alligators and crocodiles belong to one reptile family.

The tuatara belongs to its own reptile group.

Snakes and lizards make up the fourth reptile family.

Ancient animals

Sea turtles have been on Earth for over 200 million years—since the time dinosaurs lived. Long ago, their **ancestors** lived on land but started spending more time in the ocean. Over millions of years, the feet of the sea turtle ancestors turned into flippers, and their bodies became more **streamlined**, or smoothly shaped.

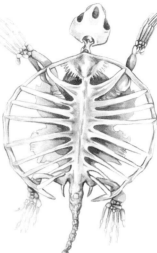

The skeleton shown here is that of a sea turtle ancestor called Archelon. It is about two million years old, and it is so huge that two cars could fit between its front flippers!

snapping turtle

- Turtles cannot see or hear well, but sea turtles have excellent hearing and can see well under water and in the dark.

- Turtles have clawed feet. Some can swim well, but a sea turtle is made for swimming! The sea turtle's flippers and streamlined body allow it to swim long distances at fast speeds.

Turtle or sea turtle?

Turtles and sea turtles are different in many ways. Below are some differences.

- A turtle can pull its body into its shell, but a sea turtle cannot.

- Turtles live both on land and in water, but sea turtles are **marine** reptiles that live only in the ocean.

green sea turtle

Different sea turtles

There are more than 260 **species**, or kinds, of turtles. There are only seven species of sea turtles. They are shown on these two pages. Sea turtles vary in size, color, and shape. Although they differ in appearance, they have similar habits and behaviors.

All sea turtles have flat, stream-lined shells, except the leatherback sea turtle, which has no shell at all. Most sea turtles have strong jaws with sharp ridges for tearing off bits of food. They have no teeth because they swallow their food whole.

*Ridleys are about 24 inches (60 cm) long and weigh less than 100 pounds (45 kg). The Kemp's ridley, left, is the most **endangered** sea turtle. The olive ridley sea turtle, right, is also endangered.*

*The hawksbill is named after the shape of its jaw, which looks like the beak of a hawk. This turtle is three feet (90 cm) long and weighs over 100 pounds (45 kg). Its shell has over-lapping brown **scutes**, or scales. In the past, people hunted the hawksbill for its beautiful shell, from which they made jewelry and other gift items. There are not many hawksbill sea turtles left!*

(right) The Australian flatback sea turtle is just over three feet (90 cm) long. It weighs under 200 pounds (90 kg) and lives only in Australia and Papua, New Guinea.

2 nails

(left) The loggerhead sea turtle has two nails on its front flippers and five scutes on each side of its shell. It looks similar to the green sea turtle below, but the green sea turtle has four scutes on each side of its body and one nail on each front flipper. Both turtles are about four feet (1 m) long and weigh from 100 to 450 pounds (45 to 203 kg).

5 scutes

4 scutes

1 nail

The leatherback is the biggest sea turtle. It can weigh 1400 pounds (636 kg) and can be more than seven feet (2 m) in length. Instead of a shell, this turtle has a rubbery back with ridges that run lengthwise down its body. The leatherback has a weak jaw—it eats mainly jellyfish. This sea turtle can live in cold, northern waters because a thick layer of fat under its skin keeps its body temperature warm, even in very cold water.

7

What is a life cycle?

All animals go through a set of changes called a **life cycle**. They are born or hatch from eggs and then grow and become adults. As adults, they make babies of their own.

adult

juvenile

eggs

hatchling

egg hatching

*adult green
sea turtle*

A sea turtle's life cycle

The life cycle of a sea turtle begins with an egg. After hatching, the baby grows into a **juvenile** and then an adult. Adult sea turtles **mate**, and the females lay eggs. With each egg that hatches, a new life cycle starts.

A life span

A **life span** is different from a life cycle. A life span is the length of time an animal lives. Sea turtles in the wild can live to 100 years, but few survive to be more than 50!

9

Finding that beach!

The life cycle of every sea turtle starts on a beach, which is where females lay eggs. A female must lay her eggs on land, but she will not lay them just anywhere. There is only one place she will lay her eggs—the same beach where she hatched! Her mother and grandmother also hatched there. Every two to three years, the female sea turtle swims back to this special beach.

Sea turtles leave the ocean to lay their eggs and then return to the ocean again.

How can a sea turtle tell?

How does a sea turtle know where it was born? No one knows how it knows! Scientists think that sea turtles may be able to find the right beach by using the positions of the moon and stars to guide them. Sea turtles might also feel the **magnetic pull** of the earth or smell certain odors that are carried by ocean **currents**.

Home at last!

When a sea turtle arrives at the right beach, she pulls herself across the sand using her flippers. She has no legs for walking and her body is heavy, but she has eggs to lay, and nothing will stop her!

Patrick Ching '98

Laying her eggs

When the turtle finds a moist spot on the beach, she starts digging an **egg chamber**, or nest, for her eggs. She uses her front flippers to clear away loose sand, and she digs the hole with her back flippers.

Many sea turtles, such as the olive ridley above, dig nests that are two feet (60 cm) deep. Most dig their nests when it is dark. The Kemp's ridley is the only sea turtle that makes her nest during the day.

Many turtle eggs

Making a nest and laying eggs is called **nesting**. After the mother sea turtle digs a nest, she lays her eggs by squeezing them out of her **cloaca**. The soft, leathery eggs are about the size of golf balls. The female lays a **clutch** of 100 to 150 eggs. A clutch is a group of eggs that hatches together. She lays many eggs to make sure that some of her babies will survive.

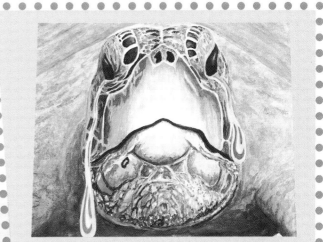

On land, the eyes of sea turtles seem to pour tears. The turtles drink ocean water and need to get rid of the extra salt in their bodies, so they "cry" it out through their eyes! They release salt in the ocean, too, but tears are harder to see in water.

Out of every 5000 eggs, only one will end up as an adult sea turtle that will make babies.

Leaving her babies

After the mother sea turtle finishes laying her eggs, she covers them with the sand that she dug up. She throws more loose sand around the nest and presses it down with her body.

The sea turtle's job is now finished, and she heads back to the ocean. She knows which way to go, even in the dark. The sky, which appears brighter over the ocean, guides her home.

The mother sea turtle leaves her nest and goes back to her ocean home.

Dangers all around

Not all of the eggs laid by the female sea turtle will hatch. Some are carried away by floods, but most are eaten by **predators**. Raccoons, wild dogs, pigs, ghost crabs, sea birds, and several types of insects eat sea turtle eggs.

People are another threat

People also eat the eggs of sea turtles. The eggs are easy to find because the sea turtle cannot cover her tracks. The tracks are wide and resemble tractor-tire tracks. They lead people right to the sea turtle's nest!

(top) When the mother turtle was laying her eggs, she did not notice that a raccoon was watching her. As soon as she left, the raccoon went right to the nest and ate many of the eggs.

(right) The people who robbed this sea turtle nest also flipped the turtle on its back. In this position, the animal cannot move. The nest robbers will come back for it later. They will eat the sea turtle's meat and use its shell to make gifts for tourists to buy.

Inside the egg

A mother sea turtle does not look after her eggs. The sand **incubates** them, or keeps them warm. The sex of the baby turtles depends on the temperature in the nest. Warmer nests make female turtles, and cooler nests make males.

yolk sac

umbilical stalk

embryo

The **embryo**, or developing baby, grows inside the egg for 45 to 70 days. It gets food from a **yolk sac** that is connected to its body by an **umbilical stalk**. The shell of the egg is soft and full of tiny **pores**, or holes, that absorb water and air from the sand.

Breaking out!

When the embryo inside the egg is fully formed, it is ready to hatch. The baby uses the **egg tooth** on its snout to break the egg shell.

After the baby cracks the shell, it **emerges**, or comes out of the egg. The **hatchling**, or newly hatched baby, moves its flippers as if it were swimming upward through the sand. The other hatchlings also emerge and crawl up and over one another. It takes the baby turtles three days to reach the surface of the sand.

Journey to the ocean

The hatchlings are so tiny that one could easily fit in your hand. After they climb out of their nest, they start a dangerous journey to the ocean. Their shells are still soft, so they are easy prey for the dogs, birds, crabs, and raccoons that wait on the beach to eat them.

Hatchlings face many dangers on the beach. This hatchling has been grabbed by a crab.

Across the beach

At night, the hatchlings slowly make their way across the beach. They drag their bodies along the sand toward the brighter sky over the ocean—just as their mother did.

The beach may not look very wide, but it is a long distance for tiny hatchlings to travel. Only a few will make it to the ocean.

Far out at sea

The hatchlings swim quickly away from shore. They must get past the shallow waters where predators could easily grab them. The hatchlings come to the surface often to breathe because their lungs are small. They swim all night and the next day until they reach deep water. No one knows where they go next!

carapace

plastron

A turtle's top shell is dark, but its bottom shell is light. This color difference helps protect all turtles, especially juveniles such as the one below.

Countershading

In the ocean, **countershading** protects a sea turtle. From above, sea birds cannot see the sea turtle's dark **carapace** against the deep ocean water. The sea turtle is also hidden from the fish below it because its light **plastron** blends in with the bright sky.

21

Floating in weeds

A baby sea turtle grows quickly in the ocean. Its egg tooth is gone two weeks after the baby hatched. Its body grows, and its shell begins to harden. For its first year of life, the sea turtle stays in deep water and finds food in floating beds of seaweed.

The young sea turtle eats only **plankton**. Plankton is made up of tiny plants and animals that float on top of the ocean. Not only does the turtle find food in the seaweed, it also finds protection. The colors and patterns of its shell blend in with those of the sea plants.

By the end of its first year, a young sea turtle has a hard shell about the size of a dinner plate. Its shell protects its body, but sharks and dolphins still can take bites out of its flippers. This tiny loggerhead sea turtle is eating a spiny lobster.

Eating adult food

At first, young turtles eat mainly plankton, but as they grow, they need to eat other kinds of foods. They return to shallower waters to find these foods.

Different diets

Different turtles have different diets. Most eat fish, fish eggs, crabs, sponges, and sea cucumbers. Leatherbacks stay far out in the ocean, where they hunt jellyfish in deep waters. Green sea turtles, shown below and right, eat mostly sea grasses, but they also eat small shellfish, jellyfish, and sponges.

Robert Tho

Back to the beach

Between the ages of 15 and 20 female sea turtles are ready to make babies, but some wait until they are 50! They swim to the nesting sites to meet up with the males and mate with them. The males **fertilize** the eggs of the females with their **sperm**. Only fertilized eggs can become babies.

A female can lay her eggs two weeks later or store a male's sperm in her body for several months. When it is time to lay her eggs, she starts a long journey called **migration** back to the beach where she hatched. During migration, she does not eat. She lives off the fat stored in her body.

A new life cycle begins

A female sea turtle may not lay any eggs for two or three years. She may then lay six clutches of eggs in one season.

After laying a clutch, the sea turtle returns to the water for several days before laying the next one. When an egg hatches, a new life cycle begins.

Sea turtles in danger

Sea turtles face many dangers in the ocean and on land. Today there are fewer sea turtles than ever before! Some species are **extinct**, and most are endangered.

Going toward the light

The nesting areas of many sea turtles are gone or are part of tourist resorts. The bright lights of the hotels confuse nesting turtles trying to find the ocean.

Instead of heading toward the ocean, the sea turtles go toward the hotel lights. Some are run over by cars as they cross roads near the hotels. Hatchlings are also confused by the lights as they try to make their way to the sea.

Baby turtles can be confused by hotel lights and head the wrong way!

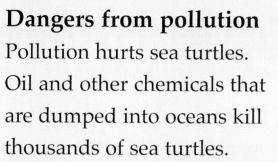

Dangers from pollution

Pollution hurts sea turtles. Oil and other chemicals that are dumped into oceans kill thousands of sea turtles.

Garbage at sea

Sea turtles that eat jellyfish often mistake balloons and plastic bags for their favorite food. When they eat these objects, they choke on them.

Cigarettes kill turtles, too!

Cigarette butts on beaches are washed into oceans, and sea turtles mistake them for food. Cigarettes contain poisons that stay in the bodies of sea turtles and eventually kill them.

*One serious health problem for the green sea turtle in Hawaii is **fibropapilloma**. This **virus** causes tumors to grow on the head, neck, and eyes of the sea turtle. The tumors make it difficult for the animal to see, move, or look for food. Scientists think that the virus may be caused by chemicals that are being dumped into the ocean. What can you do to help?* *See page 30.*

How you can help

You can help sea turtles by learning as much as you can about them. When you learn about them, you will realize that they are **prehistoric** wonders! You will not want them to disappear from the Earth.

You can help by asking your parents and friends not to use harmful chemical cleaners and **pesticides** in their homes. These chemicals eventually end up in the oceans, where they hurt and kill sea turtles.

Get the message across

To understand sea turtles, write your own book about these ancient reptiles. In your book, include an adventure story about a hatchling's trip to the sea or write a poem about this dangerous journey!

Adopting a beach or turtle

If you live near the ocean, you and your classmates can adopt a beach and help clean it up. No matter where you live, you can raise money to adopt a beach, sea turtle, or other endangered animal. Visit these websites to find out how you can help:
www.worldwildlife.org
www.aloha.net/~wild/turtle
WWW.PACIFICWHALE.ORG

Ask your parents if there are any wildlife parks where you could visit sea turtles to learn about how amazing they really are. The children in the pictures on these pages are learning about how they can help sea turtles. On page 30, they are moving hatchlings to the ocean. The boy on this page is also working with a sea-turtle rescue group. The two children above are getting to know a green sea turtle.

Glossary

current A steady flow of ocean water that is caused by the earth's magnetic pull

endangered Describing an animal species that is in danger of dying out

extinct Describing an animal species that no longer exists on Earth

fertlize To add sperm to an egg so it can form a baby inside

magnetic pull Describing the force that causes a magnet to point either to the North Pole or to the South Pole

marine Describing an animal that lives in the ocean

mate (v) To join together to make babies; (n) a mating partner

migrate To travel long distances in search of food or better weather

pesticides Chemicals made to kill insects

predator An animal that hunts and eats other animals

prehistoric Describing animals that existed before the beginning of recorded history

species Within a larger group of animals, a smaller group that has the same bodies and habits; for example, leatherbacks are a species of sea turtle

sperm A male reproductive cell that joins with a female's egg to produce babies

virus A tiny organism that lives off plants, animals, or people and causes disease

Index

6 7 8 9 0   Printed in the U.S.A.   0 9 8 7 6